The Wrong Place

poems by

Tawn Parent

Finishing Line Press
Georgetown, Kentucky

The Wrong Place

Copyright © 2024 by Tawn Parent
ISBN 979-8-88838-671-2 First Edition
All rights reserved under International and Pan-American Copyright Conventions. No part of this book may be reproduced in any manner whatsoever without written permission from the publisher, except in the case of brief quotations embodied in critical articles and reviews.

ACKNOWLEDGMENTS

I would like to thank the following publications for publishing individual pieces:
Tipton Poetry Journal: "The Wrong Place"
Home Planet News Online: "Trial by Fire," "Crimson Gold," "Age of Reason," "Ready to Fly," "The Magic Cooler," and "Moment of Truth"
Anti-Heroin Chic: "Unrecognizable" and "Game Night"
Nzuri: "Vanishing Point"
Flying Island Journal: "The Plaid Blanket"
Ignite Studio Art, Poetry, and Short Story Anthology: "Trial by Fire" and "Ready to Fly"
Gal's Guide Anthology: "Wishes," "Crimson Gold," and "The Magic Cooler"
Elevation Review: "False Advertising"

My gratitude also goes to my friend and writer Lisa Hendrickson, for giving me the kick in the pants I needed to start down this road, and to gifted poet and teacher Lylanne Musselman, who encouraged and shaped my work, and made me believe that my efforts were publishable. I owe a debt of thanks to the following physicians: Mark Cain, Emily Mueller, Cristiana Hentea, and Amy Wilson at Riley Hospital; Jeffrey Buchsbaum at IU Health; Ammar Hayani and Sharad Salvi at Lurie Children's Hospital; and John Chang at Northwestern Medicine Proton Center, as well as many nurses and other practitioners at all those facilities. They helped bring us through to the other side. I thank my husband, Steve, and daughter, Ruby, for their love, support, and patience. Most of all I thank my son, Eli, who was forced, with no roadmap, to lead us on our cancer journey, and who did so with a fierce determination I had not imagined possible. I want to be like him when I grow up.

Publisher: Leah Huete de Maines
Editor: Christen Kincaid
Cover Art: Ganna Gonen
Author Photo: Steve Spicklemire
Cover Design: Elizabeth Maines McCleavy

Order online: www.finishinglinepress.com
also available on amazon.com

Author inquiries and mail orders:
Finishing Line Press
PO Box 1626
Georgetown, Kentucky 40324
USA

Contents

Thanksgiving Surprise 1
Aftermath 2
The Wrong Place 4
Trading Up 6
A Side of Red Tears 7
Cold Comfort 9
Vanishing Point 10
Christmas Motions 11
The First Day 13
False Advertising 15
Transformation 17
Age of Reason 18
The Magic Cooler 20
Alone Time 21
The Plaid Blanket 22
Sleep Tight 23
Unfriended 24
Wee Hours Rendezvous 25
Wishes 27
The Anti-Nausea Dance 29
Unrecognizable 30
Good Luck Charm? 31
Game Night 32
New Bedtime Routine 33
Challenge Coin 34
Crimson Gold 36
A Turn for the Worse 37
Sweet 16 39
Moment of Truth 40
Trial by Fire 41
Battle with the Bulge 42
Back in the Swing 44
Every Three Months 45
Shadow Christmas 46
Missing Person 47
Ready to Fly 48

For Eli, the brave

Thanksgiving Surprise

Thanksgiving morning,
young Eli wakes up
not feeling good.
Friday, he runs a fever.
Saturday, back pain.
Off to the urgent care with dad.
Maybe kidney stones?
Sent to the hospital for an MRI.
Moved to the children's hospital
for more tests.
Sunday, a mass in the kidney,
surgery tomorrow,
probably cancer.

And just like that,
the holidays
and life as we know it
are over.

Aftermath

The surgery went off
without a hitch.
The next day
Eli's *resting comfortably,*
as they say,
when his eyes fly open.

Ow! he says. *My stomach.*
I call for the nurse.
*Some discomfort after surgery
is normal*, she says.
But the pain gets worse.
Eli's eyes squeeze shut against it.
Isn't there something you can do?
I plead.
The nurse offers to check with the doctor.

Eli's fists are clenched.
He throws me a panicked look.
Not knowing what to do,
I stroke his arm and murmur
I'm here, over and over,
a desperate mantra,
for what feels like forever.

Eventually a different nurse arrives,
dims the lights,
and gives Eli a pain pill.
I rest my cheek against Eli's,
clutch his hand,
as he chews his lips,
and wait
for the suffering to end.

Finally I feel him relax.
Better? I ask
He nods.
Soon he drifts to sleep,
his brow unfurrowed.

I stumble into the bathroom,
my whole body heaving
with long-suppressed sobs,
and collapse against the sink.

The Wrong Place

I don't think we're in the right place,
my son said,
looking up at the sign above the desk.
What's oncology? he asked.
It was my turn to look up at Eli,
(my tall manboy with the baby face),
into those wondering hazel eyes.
My tongue curled around the word,
reluctant to release its awful power.
Big breath.
It means cancer, I said.

My husband came in from the parking lot
and we three trooped down a hall,
into a small room,
without enough space to breathe,
sat in hard plastic chairs,
and heard from an unsmiling doctor,
aggressive, unusual,
large tumor, sarcoma,
blood in the belly,
more detailed pathology,
bone marrow biopsy,
bone scan, body scan,
port-o-cath, clinical trials,
chemotherapy, radiation,
nausea, vomiting, losing hair,
treatment before Christmas,
no more school this year.

No school! Eli exclaimed,
as if that were the worst of the news.
But perhaps it was the only bit he could grasp
in the soup of this surreal conversation.
We sat and stared,
dry-eyed and numb,
nodded, signed, took appointment cards
into helpless hands,
and slowly rose.

Our legs somehow carried us
from the small room,
back down the hall
and out of that right and wrong place
into the gray afternoon.

Trading Up

Without so much as a
How are you feeling?
to Eli,
just home from surgery,
Dr. S. launched,
in his ungentle
and discompassionate way,
into a litany
of the scariest news imaginable.

After that first meeting,
it was clear Dr. S. had to go.
I could not envision
this comfort-less clinician
walking alongside us
through our darkest days.
No, my son deserved better.

We soon found our way
to Dr. M. and Dr. H.
They greeted Eli,
asked about his interests,
and immediately cast his case
in a more positive light.
Suddenly I could breathe again,
and my heart fluttered
with fresh hope.

Our new doctors
could not spare us
all the agony that awaited.
But thanks to their smiles
and steadfast
concern and humanity,
we did not suffer alone.

A Side of Red Tears

As my son sleeps
I slip out to the hospital lounge,
settle
into a vinyl chair
and try to ignore
the home-improvement show
playing to no one.
In my lap is the flecked, photocopied packet
that is the plan of Eli's treatment.
I must educate myself about the five drugs,
with their unpronounceable names,
that will soon be careening
through my young son's veins.

The side effects are divided
into three categories:
Likely, Less Likely, and Rare
but Serious.
Along with the usual suspects
of nausea, vomiting, and hair loss
in the Likely category
are red urine, red sweat, red saliva, and red tears.
I try to picture my son with red tears
coursing down his cheeks.
It sounds like a horror movie.
I'm glad they warned me.
I'm also grateful that
dark discoloration of the hands and feet
and loss of nails
are on the Less Likely list,
along with seizures
and gonadal dysfunction.

On to Rare but Serious,
where the real fun begins.
Here I find an abundance
of the term *life-threatening,*
which includes such outcomes
as lung damage, cardiac toxicity,

kidney failure, and coma.
But they saved the best
for last:
A new cancer or leukemia
resulting from this treatment.
So, all the misery to come,
even if successful,
could ultimately beget
more
cancer.

I put the paper down
with an unsteady hand,
and stare at the cheery
face on the screen
extolling the virtues of hickory cabinets.
I realize that I have made it through
only one of the five drugs.
But this, I decide, will do
for now.

Cold Comfort

Don't worry about losing your hair,
the surgeon told my son.
It comes back better.

Vanishing Point

It's amazing how suddenly
your life can narrow
to a single point,
like one of those drawings
that shows two parallel lines
coming together
in the distance.

The full breadth of my life
diminishes as I speed
toward that vanishing point.

My new job has receded
into the rear view,
work emails floating across
my vision like roadside signs,
seen, but not remembered.

Even my other child,
the healthy one,
the one who gets passed
from aunt to neighbor,
has drifted into left field.
She'll manage just fine,
won't she?

Fading to the right
are book club, dinners out,
volunteer work, yoga,
and haircuts,
all inconsequential
as I fix my eyes
on the one thing
that absolutely, positively
cannot vanish.

Christmas Motions

This year we'll break tradition.
Forget about driving into the country,
listening to Bing Crosby Christmas tunes,
with hot chocolate in the thermos,
to cut down our own tree.
Forget tromping around the farm,
cheerfully arguing about the height, fullness,
or attractive shape of this or that tree.
This one's too crooked.
Look at the bare spot in that one.
Blue spruce? Such a pretty color,
but the needles are so sharp!
White pines have soft needles,
and that classic look,
but what limp branches!
The ornaments always fall.
Shall we compromise
with a Fraser fir?

This year there will be none of that.
Between doctor appointments,
there is no time.
Besides, Eli is too weak,
and who can muster the enthusiasm?
We just drive to the hardware store
and grab the first one we see.
Not as fragrant as a fresh-cut tree,
but who will notice?

Decorating the tree
is normally an all-day affair,
as we sip cider
and reminisce about the origins
of each ornament.
Look at this one that
Ruby made in preschool.
What was Grandma thinking,
giving us this gaudy one?
Remember picking this one out

that time we went to the mountains?
Hello Kitty? Please!

This year I force a smile
as we hang the tinsel.
Eli, wan, lies on the couch, watching.
His first chemo cycle begins soon.
Will his hair last until Christmas?
The whole ritual feels off.
All I can think of is,
will this be the last time
that we trim the tree together?
Later I tell my husband,
If the worst happens,
we have to go away next year.
I can't be here, doing this,
without him.

The First Day

I do not wake my son. His endless day will begin soon enough. Eventually he stumbles from his room and remembers what day it is: Day One of a new round of treatment. He groans, then blows out a noisy whoosh of air. Then groans and sighs again, these alternating sounds all the lamentation my teenage boy will allow himself.

He forces down a hearty breakfast, knowing it may be his last good meal for days.

I apply lidocaine cream to his implanted port, numbing it for the assault to come, and cover it with plastic food wrap. Packing is a quick affair: mostly fleece pants and long-sleeved undershirts, with buttons at the top to allow access to his port.

We head to the hospital in the late morning and I drop him off at the front door. I remember our first time here. In the waiting room was a boy of about 12, skinny, bald, and hauling an IV pole around. Later I wept, believing I could not bear to see my son become thus. But now my own skinny, bald son, wearing his yellow face mask, heads up to the oncology clinic while I park the car. I load our small bags into one of the fleet of blood-red wagons in the lobby and join Eli inside. The receptionist snaps on Eli's hospital bracelet and we settle in to wait.

We are called back to a tiny room, where a nurse takes his vitals. I hold my breath when he steps on the scale, mentally nudging the blue numbers higher. Then we move to another room, where a nurse starts an IV. "First stick of the day," Eli remarks with a smirk. He stands up and suddenly—oof!—my tall boy is in my arms. I had always pictured a faint like a crumple, but Eli falls like a tree. A nurse calls out and people come bustling in, bearing juice boxes and crackers. Eli comes to, wondering what all the fuss is about.

Eventually the nurses leave us. I shift in the uncomfortable chair as we wait for an available room. An hour later, our escort arrives. Eli pulls his IV pole and I pull the wagon as we wind down hospital corridors, up the elevator, and onto the cancer floor. Here, Eli can finally take off his mask, because of the unit's special air-purification system.

From the wagon I unload our bags, the stuffed green monkey that will hang from Eli's IV pole, and the yellow tub of candy that I hope he will feel good enough to dig into. I put it in a tempting spot just under the TV, its ridiculous smiley face radiating hope that the nausea will be manageable this time. I used to load it up with his favorite chocolates, but Eli has lost the taste for it. Today the little bucket is bursting with gummy worms and Laffy Taffy.

This afternoon is the only tolerable part of the stay. Later the nurses will come in wearing their crunchy haz-mat suits and face shields to protect themselves from the toxins they unleash into my son's veins. But first, they must pump his body with fluids. (The doctors want to poison him, but not too much.) As the IV does its thing, we head to the playroom for some air hockey. Too soon the misery will begin, but for now, it's game on!

False Advertising

*Each chemo cycle will require
a three-day hospital stay,*
they told us.
But severe nausea
stretched Eli's first stay
to six days,
when he was mercifully released
on Christmas Eve.

Now it's cycle two, day eight,
with no end in sight.
The new nausea drug,
in a patch behind his ear,
made him so sleepy
that he woke up only long enough
to go to the bathroom.
One time Eli was so confused
that he tried to wash his hands
in the laundry cart.

But he wasn't eating,
so off came the patch,
and in swooped the nausea.
The doctors keep mixing up
different cocktails,
but still no magic potion.
Eli vomits and vomits and vomits.
After five days without food,
he mournfully looks
up from his bed
and says, *I just want
some of Nonna's noodles.*
When his 5'11" frame
falls to 100 pounds,
they start IV nutrition.

Next comes fever,
then diarrhea,
then C. diff,

then mucositis,
then kidney dysfunction.

Now we've been here two weeks
and Eli feels worse than ever.
So I want to know,
since we didn't get our three-day hospital stay,
could we please get a refund?

Transformation

No hanging out in the waiting room
for Eli. He is whisked
straight into a private exam room,
where everyone is masked and ready.

The doctor gets right to work,
cutting, pulling, and prodding.
After half an hour,
his job is done.

How does it feel? he asks.
Eli grins, swirling his tongue
around his now metal-free teeth.

His head may be bald
and his body too lean,
but oh, what a dazzling smile!

Age of Reason

What is the best age
for a child to have cancer?
Should I be grateful
that my boy was stricken
when he was old enough
to understand?

On the cancer ward,
I watch the other children,
the sobbing babies,
in their uncomprehending agony;
the giggling toddlers
in the bright red wagons;
the preschoolers
who drive around in plastic cars,
as their parents follow,
pulling their IV poles;
the 7-year-olds struggling
with their schoolwork.

For them, the distress vanishes
with the pain.
There is no dread of the next time,
and the next time,
and the prospect
of no next time.

Around come the volunteer
who performs magic tricks
and the chirpy homework helper,
who offer my child
no solace at all.

He is one of the teens,
who do their best to look cool
(in spite of their baldness and frailty)
and ignore each other
as they pace the halls,
ravaged

both by chemo
and the knowledge
of exactly
what they're up against.

The Magic Cooler

On our porch
sits an old green metal cooler,
placed there by a friend.
It holds treasures.

After a long day
wrangling with insurance,
open the cooler
and presto—
chicken pot pie!

Coming home
from a surprise blood transfusion,
open the cooler—
vegetable soup for dinner!

White blood cell counts at zero,
praying to avoid infection,
open the cooler—
mac and cheese from scratch,
Eli's favorite!

Homemade delights
from unseen hands,
filling us with warmth and love,
day after delicious day—
magic!

Alone Time

No visitors, Eli tells us
from his hospital bed.
*I just want to sit here
with no one talking to me.*
He retreats into his private hell,
where even his parents
are denied entry.

The Plaid Blanket

I cover my son with the fuzzy plaid blanket
I bought spontaneously on Christmas Eve,
spying it out of the edge of my eye
at the grocery checkout, of all places.
Something bright
to break up the chilly whiteness of the hospital bed
and offer a scrap of hominess
in the stern, ringing room.
The fleece provides warmth
that the thin, sterile hospital blankets can't match,
no matter how many you pile on.

At home the plaid blanket
lives in a shopping bag,
packed and ready
for when fever sends us running to the ER.
Then I lift the folded softness from the brown bag
and stretch it across the foot of Eli's bed
in the children's cancer ward
to claim this rolling metal island as our own.

When the blanket becomes soiled,
I hurry to the hospital laundry,
scrawl his room number in marker
on the hard lid of the washer.
Inside, the blanket
has a heyday,
sharing its colorful fluff
with all its neighbors
as they churn together in the sudsy water.
Pants, shirts, and socks emerge
covered in red, green, and white fuzz,
small bits of comfort
clinging to Eli's clothes
like homespun snow.

Sleep Tight

I yawn and rub my neck.
It's 10 p.m., and I'm ready
to stretch out
on my narrow cot
beside Eli's hospital bed
and attempt to sleep.
Time for bed, I say.
His eyes glued to his laptop screen,
Eli replies, *I want to finish my movie.*

I tilt my head, considering.
I have always stayed up
until my kids were tucked in.

Parenting a child with cancer
has meant throwing out
so many rules.
*Play on the computer
as much as you like!
Eat whatever you want
whenever you're hungry!*
But for some reason
I don't want to let this one go.
I want to see him sleeping
peacefully,
to reduce by one
my many worries
before I shut my eyes.

But need it matter so much?
The nurse has come in,
overhearing our conversation.
I promise you, she says with a grin,
sweeping an arm across
Eli's tubes, wires, and monitors,
*if he tries to make a run for it,
he won't get far.*
She has a point.

Unfriended, After Cancer Diagnosis

Even texts from Eli's friends
have stopped.
Too much and too little to say.
Cul8r?

Wee Hours Rendezvous

Among the tasks
I never imagined for myself
is giving intravenous drugs
to my son.
Yet here I am.

At 4 a.m. I lay out supplies—
syringes and alcohol wipes—
for the first dose of the day.
Kneeling on the floor by his bed,
in the moody light of the lamp,
I don the blue nitrile gloves,
rip a stiff foil package,
remove the small, damp, acrid square
and scrub the tip
of the catheter tail
protruding from his implanted port,
for the requisite 15 seconds.

Slowly I pull a saline syringe
from its crinkly package
so as not to wake him,
uncap it and pull back
on the plunger,
holding the syringe close
to my sleepy eyes,
and then push it until I see
a tiny drip pop out of the end,
because an air bubble
in the bloodstream
could mean death.
I click open the catheter lock,
screw in the syringe
and push in 5 ml,
just half, not the whole barrel,
to flush the line.

After unscrewing that first syringe,
I inject the antibiotic,

steady and sure.
Then more saline, the other half.
Then a shot of Heparin
to keep the blood from clotting.
So many dangers
in this brief procedure.
I remove the last syringe,
rub the port cap
with another alcohol wipe
while I count to 15,
click the catheter lock back in place.

My mission accomplished,
I release a long breath,
gather up the refuse,
and stuff it in the square, red sharps box.
I tiptoe from the room
and head back to bed
until the alarm wakes me
to do it all again.

Wishes

We'd like to refer Eli to Make-A-Wish,
the social worker told me.
Oh, I replied,
unsure whether to be pleased
or worried.
My sister had the same reaction.
After I shared the news,
a long pause.
It doesn't mean he's terminal,
I said. *It just means
he has a critical illness.*
Oh! she replied.
Well, that's good, right?
So many awkward
conversations in this business.

Then it was Eli's turn to contemplate.
What did he want more than anything?
To do, to be, to meet, to go …
Watch the Saints play in the Superdome?
Meet his favorite Cubs player?
Paint the Big Apple red?
What a relief to lose himself in fantasy.

Make a wish—
a tantalizing prospect.
I thought about mine.
That my son was spending his days
at school
instead of in the hospital.
That he could still relate
to his friends' preoccupations
with Saturday's game
or the cute girl in chemistry.
That Eli was thinking about college,
not the result of his next blood test.
That he could ever go back
to being who he was
before.

In the end, Eli picked Colorado,
a ski vacation.
The trip was perfect.
The limo ride to the airport
for our family's first flight together,
without a worry
about traffic or parking.
The royal treatment
wherever we went.
The luxurious condo
just steps from the slopes.
The horse-drawn sleigh ride
through the mountains.
The skating rink encircled
by tall pines and snowy peaks.
The chance to drive a sled
pulled by huskies.
The historic town all lit up,
like a fairy tale.
Eli's dazzling wish came true.

I smiled through it all,
trying not to regret
that mine did not.

The Anti-Nausea Dance

Mom, I have to pee!
my son calls from his hospital bed.
He has waited until the last moment
because even the smell of his chemo-tainted urine
makes him puke.
I shake off sleep and jump up,
launching into the retch-prevention routine:
Spray Cinnamon Glade in the bathroom,
pop a Wintergreen Life Saver into Eli's mouth,
smear VapoRub on the inside of a surgical mask
and loop it behind his ears.

Will it all be enough to stave off nausea,
to preserve the precious meal just consumed,
the ounces he cannot afford to lose?
I grab the IV pole and steer him into the bathroom,
crack the door and stand outside,
clutching a pink vomit tub,
just in case.

Eli makes quick work of it,
urinating into a plastic bottle
that the nurse will measure later.
He pulls up his blue sweatpants
as he shouts, "Done!"
I throw open the door,
take hold of the IV pole
and whisk him from the bathroom.
OK? I ask.
He nods.

Success!
I fall back into the chair-come-bed,
a smile briefly tugging at my lips.
After an arduous day,
I cannot help but savor
this small triumph.

Unrecognizable

Is this my son,
this boy who towers over me
but who I now outweigh?
His solid frame
of two months ago
has withered.
I can feel his ribs
when we hug.

Is this my son,
who ran so fast
and jumped so high,
but who can now
barely climb the stairs?

Is this my son
with smudgy rings
around lashless eyes,
which have a faraway look
that never goes away?

Is this my son
whose once-hairy legs
are now as smooth as a baby's?
And like a baby,
I now tend him around the clock.

This teen, with his life
of friends, card games,
and ultimate Frisbee,
cruising toward adulthood,
suddenly entered freefall
and landed back in my arms.

No parties or field trips,
no joking around in history class.
Just hospital to home and back again,
glides this shadow
who my son
has become.

Good Luck Charm?

My yellow silicone bracelet says, *Sarcoma*.
Never a superstitious person,
I now wear it always,
even in the shower,
so my skin is constantly in contact
with a symbol of my son's illness,
as if I needed to be reminded.

I am aware
of the ridiculousness
of taking comfort in a trinket.
Yet I'm unwilling to remove it,
as if that simple act could betray
my love
and provoke the gods.

Game Night

At home, evenings playing cards at the game shop are a Friday night ritual. My son Eli is one of the regulars, known, comfortable in the stuffy room alive with competition, laughter, and the funk of young male bodies. Often, he wins and returns home beaming, his wallet a bit thicker than when he left.

Now we aren't home, but in Chicago for two dismal months of daily radiation treatments. It's the latest upheaval in Eli's three-month-old tangle with cancer. Staying at the Ronald McDonald House means being removed from every semblance of his normal life: home, school, friends, family, and his beloved card game.

Life here has the regimentation of prison life: Wake up, shower, swallow cereal in the communal dining room, study for three hours, down a quick lunch, drive to the Proton Center. Avoid eye contact with the other patients awaiting their punishment. Lie completely still for an impossible 30 minutes as the technicians zap his midsection with painful rays. Not a sneeze. Not a twitch. Stock. Still.

Back to the Ronald McDonald House. Collapse into a nap. Wake up groggy. Try to find a quiet corner of the busy dining room at dinner to avoid the constant prattle about medical procedures, side effects, and setbacks.

Desperate for a break from the joyless routine, for a chance to feel like his sharp, humorous 15-year-old self, Eli scopes out game nights in the area, finds one 40 minutes away. *But you won't know anyone,* I caution. *And you'll have to wear your face mask.*

I know, he says. *Let's go.* He loads his red backpack with small boxes of cards and we set off. Eli is quiet in the car. Three highways and a tollbooth later, we pull into a parking lot with a cluster of cars near the door of a glass-fronted game shop, the only lights in the otherwise empty shopping center.

Eli pulls his knit Cubs hat over his bald head and dons his yellow mask. *Call me,* I say as he gets out of the car. *Yeah,* he mutters, dismissing me with a nod, and hoists his backpack onto his bony shoulder.

My stomach tightens as I watch him stride determinedly across the dark parking lot. I can hardly stand to witness the possible failure of his quest. He walks in, stops to speak with the plaid-shirted guy behind the counter. Is it my imagination, or are people looking up at the gangly teen in the stocking cap? Eli scans the room full of strangers, eyes an available player in the corner, and approaches him. The young man peers through his long hair at my pale, skinny son, nods. Eli sits down, pulls out his cards, and begins to play.

New Bedtime Routine

After dinner at the Ronald McDonald House,
where I urge my son to eat meat
and polish off some ice cream
to keep his calories up,
I make sure he's met
his fluid intake goal.
Refill the water bottle
for tomorrow,
put it in the mini-fridge.
Top off the humidifier
and turn it on high.
Offer Eli an anti-nausea pill.
Then gently apply lotion
to his radiation burn,
the skin that will remain
discolored and vulnerable
for the rest of his life.

Before cancer struck,
bedtime kisses
had ended long ago.
But now I plant one on his cheek
every
single
night.

Challenge Coin

To mark the completion
of 31 grueling radiation treatments,
the proton team presents Eli
with a brass challenge coin
in a blue velvet box.

Eli bounces the disc
in his hand,
feeling its weight.
It is like his father's
from the Air Force Academy,
yet not.

Emblazoned with the Chicago skyline,
Eli's medallion bears
his own patient number,
an image of a patient
surrounded by caregivers,
and the word, *Believe.*

The military-inspired coin
symbolizes Eli's victory
over an enemy that is
indiscriminate, quick,
silent, and deadly,
reads the note from the team.
The medal recognizes Eli's
strength and valor
and offers courage
for what lies ahead.

I look at Eli's puffy face,
wondering,
Does he feel strong and brave?
Will this piece of metal,
however generously bestowed,
offer him true comfort,
or is it a mere token?

All four military branches
issue challenge coins.
Service members consider them
a sort of good luck charm.

Good luck I will take
for my son,
a veteran,
at age 15.

Crimson Gold

Who knew cancer patients
went through so much blood?

In some countries
family members
must walk the streets
begging for donors.
But I can rest easy,
knowing that each time
my son's blood pressure sinks,
or his labs come back low,
bags of that essential fluid
will keep showing up
from somewhere.
I long ago lost count
of how much Eli has needed.

I think of all those
unknown, benevolent souls
who have saved Eli's life
again and again.
If only I could
reach out my hand
to thank each one
for their selfless,
impossibly precious
gift.

A Turn for the Worse

Eli awakes with a fever, barely able to rise from his bed. Infection. I quickly load the van with our pre-packed bags, and off to the ER we go. Forget today's review session for his history final next week.

At the hospital Eli is immediately ushered into an exam room and receives an IV antibiotic. Eventually he is admitted, and we move to a room on the cancer floor while we wait for the antibiotic to work its magic. As Eli gets a unit of blood, I head to the cafeteria downstairs for a bite.

Walking back down the hall toward Eli's room, I spy a cluster of doctors and nurses in blue assembled around his bed and quicken my pace. Eli's blood pressure has dropped. The docs want to give him fluids to boost it, but the bag of blood is still going in, and they can't give both blood and fluids through his implanted port at once, so they hold off.

His blood pressure does not bounce back, so they decide to start an IV. They try his arm, but the vein collapses. Then the other arm. Still no good. A painful prick into his right hand and another in his left also fail. They give up on the IV and stop the blood so he can get fluids through his port. The infusion pump won't work fast enough, so the nurses take turns pushing the saline in by hand. His BP doesn't budge.

A nurse tries another bolus of fluids, pumping so hard that she has to catch her breath. At 2 a.m. the doctor on the floor calls in a team from the ICU. Eli's fingers pick constantly at the white blankets as the doctors loom over him, discussing his condition. They decide he needs to move to intensive care. I hurriedly search for my shoes, trying not to let my son see my panic. *They just need to watch you more closely,* I tell him. I call my husband, who can't come because he's home alone with our 9-year-old daughter.

Eli is rolled downstairs and plugged into even more machines. Nothing seems right with his body. His fever is too high and his heart rate too low. A kidney marker is the highest we've ever seen. He gets a new blood pressure medicine, but the red numbers show a stubborn 94/50.

Eli is hungry but is not allowed to eat until he stabilizes. He needs both platelets and hemoglobin, but his port is busy with medication. More painful needle sticks. Finally one takes in his foot, and the blood flows in.

I brush the back of my fingers over Eli's pale cheek. Amid the beeping machines, the blinking monitors, and the tattoo of my own turbulent heart, I perch at his bedside.

His diastolic dips to 43. The medicine isn't working. Eli has slipped into septic shock. My body starts to vibrate, as though it may explode.

A doctor comes by and motions me into the hall. She wastes no time with pleasantries. *Today will be the turning point,* she says. *He will either get substantially better or substantially worse. If things go south, we'll intubate him, sedate him, flood him with antibiotics, and assume control of all his bodily functions. This can happen fast, so I want you to be prepared.*

I usually pepper the doctors with questions, but in this moment I cannot summon a single word.

Sweet 16

Tears well up
as I spy out the window
a parade of balloon-toting teens
marching up the sidewalk.
Eli may have missed the class trip,
but his teacher and classmates
aren't going to miss his birthday.

You have visitors,
I call up to Eli,
whose eyes open wide
as he catches sight
of the crowd
who has come to see him.

They settle in the dining room,
break out the Hedbanz game
of *What am I?*
The headband won't fit
over Eli's stocking cap,
so he removes it,
baring his baldness
to his friends
for the first time.
No one bats an eye.

Later I peek in from the kitchen,
see Eli's face flushed with laughter.
When was the last time
I saw him laugh?

Time for cupcakes.
Happy birthday, say the friends.
We've missed you, dude.
Eli looks around the circle, beaming.
Sweet, sweet 16.

Moment of Truth

The day has come.
After one major surgery,
seven cycles of chemo,
31 radiation treatments,
and 49 days in the hospital,
the moment of truth.
Has that terrible price
been enough?

Clean scans!
Listen to the nurses cheer.
Grinning, they shout,
here is the bell,
come ring it!
Here is the giant cookie
of congratulations.
Here, here, here
is the gift
of the rest
of your life.

Trial by Fire

Amid the awfulness of cancer
arises the awesome strength
of this child who became an adult
too soon.
The source of that strength
remains a mystery.
But now that my son has looked
death in the face,
what on earth
could possibly
scare him?

The Battle with the Bulge

Under the pale flesh
of my son's upper chest
is a hard lump
where no knob should be.
The size of a clementine,
it bears a thick, crooked scar
across the top.
The mound makes Eli toss
and turn in the night,
trying to get comfortable.
Just visible under his shirt,
it is a puffy reminder
that all is not well with his body.

Before we head to the hospital,
I bathe the lump
in white numbing cream.
Round and round my fingers go,
to ease the pain
of the needle sticks to come.
Then I cover it with plastic wrap,
like a biscuit.
Nurses use the implanted port
to inject the chemo drugs
that Eli gets every three weeks.
The port is also tapped
to provide extra blood,
needed fluids,
or antibiotics.

Finally,
after seven long months,
the services of the port
are no longer required.
The surgery to remove it
is Eli's farewell kiss
to cancer treatment.
Now the scar has grown,
but the bulge is gone,

and he can sleep in peace
once more.

Back in the Swing

After nine months away,
the first day of school never felt so good.

Eli slides into his uniform khakis and polo,
almost forgotten in the back of the closet.
With his hair grown back just in time,
he tosses the faithful stocking cap in a drawer.

He wonders how he'll like the new math teacher,
contemplates his next driving lesson.
Back up to his fighting weight,
he thinks of trying out for cross-country.

Life slips back into familiar rhythms.
May the beat go on.

Every Three Months

We now live our lives
in three-month increments.
Anxiety bears down
as testing day approaches,
7 days,
6, 5, 4,
3, 2,
1.

On D-day we set out,
knowing in a few hours
we'll return,
either skipping
or dragging.

At the hospital
we head up the elevator
to the place where it all began.
Feel those excruciating memories
wash over us.
Eli pees in a cup,
gets a needle in the arm,
slides into the tube for the CAT scan.
Then the endless wait.

We try to read the doctor's expression
as she arrives.
Does she hesitate at the door?
Is she smiling with sympathy
or good news?
Will this day send Eli
back into a spiral
of drugs, nausea, pain, and fear,
or will it buy us freedom
for another three months?

Shadow Christmas

This time last year
I feared the worst,
that we'd be celebrating
the holiday without my son.

Now the day is here
and Eli is here,
living, breathing, laughing.
So why do I feel blue?

Why do I keep imagining
that he's not really here,
as I walk through a parallel
what-if life
that is the stuff
of nightmares?

Why does delight
stick in my throat,
and dread
squeeze my heart,
as if I can't quite trust
what is before my eyes?
As if unbridled joy
is too risky.

Better to temper
my feelings,
allow the ghost
of my unsurviving son
to creep around the edges
of our gathering.

I am not strong enough
to brave another fall.

Missing Person

With the nightmare of cancer
behind you
and the prospect
of an organ transplant ahead,
your life has changed
utterly.

Oh, Eli,
who will you be now?
And who might you
have been?

Ready to Fly

A year ago you were in the ICU.
Now you're visiting colleges.
Colorado or New York?
You crave an adventure
far from the home
where you spent
too much unplanned time.

My heart swells with pride
that you have the courage
to voyage out and start anew.
Yet my heart also contracts
with fear.
At 15,
you suddenly became
like a toddler again,
as for months
I monitored every aspect
of your being:
weight, temperature,
blood pressure, calories,
fluids in, fluids out.
Always just
an arm's reach away.

Once treatment ended,
you snapped right back
to your adolescent self,
racing to rejoin your friends,
as I stood by
suddenly empty-handed.

Now your limitless future beckons,
a prospect that once seemed
impossible.
Fly, Eli, fly!
If only I can bear
to let go
of your wings.

A native and resident of Indianapolis, **Parent** has been a professional writer and editor for 30 years. Her poetry and essays have appeared in *Tipton Poetry Journal, Last Stanza Poetry Journal, Home Planet News Online, Anti-Heroin Chic, Flying Island Journal, Nzuri,* and *Elevation Review,* as well as in *Gal's Guide Anthology* and *Ignite Studio Art, Poetry, and Short Story Anthology.* She has worked for various business publications, and also served as proofreader for several books. She holds a B.A. in journalism and French from Indiana University and a master's degree in English language acquisition from Marian University. She teaches English as a new language at a public elementary school. She is married with two children.

www.ingramcontent.com/pod-product-compliance
Lightning Source LLC
Chambersburg PA
CBHW020343170426
43200CB00006B/486